IN NEARBY BUSHES

Kei Miller was born in Jamaica in 1978 and has written several books across a range of genres. His 2014 collection, *The Cartographer Tries to Map a Way to Zion*, won the Forward Prize for Best Collection while his 2017 Novel, *Augustown*, won the Bocas Prize for Caribbean Literature, the Prix Les Afriques, and the Prix Carbet de la Caraïbe et du Tout-Monde. He is also an award-winning essayist. In 2010, the Institute of Jamaica awarded him the Silver Musgrave medal for his contributions to Literature and in 2018 he was awarded the Anthony Sabga medal for Arts & Letters. Kei has an MA in Creative Writing from Manchester Metropolitan University and a PhD in English Literature from the University of Glasgow. He has taught at the Universities of Glasgow, Royal Holloway and Exeter. He is the 2019 Ida Beam Distinguished Visiting Professor to the University of Iowa and is a Fellow of the Royal Society of Literature.

T0266566

IN
NEARBY
BUSHES

KEI MILLER

CARCANET

First published in Great Britain in 2019 by
Carcanet
Alliance House, 30 Cross Street
Manchester M2 7AQ
www.carcanet.co.uk

A CIP catalogue record for this book is
available from the British Library.
ISBN 978 1 78410 845 8

Book design by Andrew Latimer
Printed in Great Britain by SRP Ltd, Exeter, Devon

The publisher acknowledges financial
assistance from Arts Council England.

CONTENTS

3. IN NEARBY BUSHES

IN NEARBY BUSHES

'… the criminal a get way with a whole heap a badniss and your police neva seem to be able to catch them. Dem always escaping in nearby bushes. Tell them fi go inna the bush and catch them if a so it go.'

JAMAICAN BLOGGER, PAUL TOMLINSON, WRITING TO THE NEW COMMISSIONER OF POLICE

'I make a distinction between "the nearby bushes" and "in the nearby bushes". Perhaps it is my corrupt imagination. "In the nearby bushes" equals concealment, danger, while "the nearby bushes" equals a place of opportunity to do what one wishes to be hidden from others – sex, dispose of waste be it bodily waste or household waste.'

PROF ANTHONY HARRIOTT, DIRECTOR INSTITUTE OF CRIMINAL JUSTICE & SECURITY, UWI MONA, JAMAICA

HERE WHERE ONCE LAY THE BODIES

of

Lindel Williams (41 years old, body found September 21, 2007)
Chevaughn White (22 years old, body found December 25, 2011)
Dwayne Jones (16 years old, body found July 22, 2013)

Gary Lewis (age unreported, body found on Dec 6, 2014)
Randy Hentzel (48 years old, body found May 1, 2016)
Harold Nichols (53 years old, body found May 1, 2016)

Tanijah Howell (35 years old, body found February 18, 2017)
James Miller (age unreported, body found May 14, 2017)
Randal Riley (16 years old, body found June 2, 2017)

Christopher Williams (28 years old, body found June 2, 2017)
Desiree Gibbon (26 years old, body found November 26, 2017)
Petrice Portious (21 years old, body found February 26, 2018)

Joyan Myrie (21 years old, body found May 2, 2018)
Kadijah Saunders (9 years old, body found June 5, 2018)
Kimone Campbell (25 years old, body found June 9, 2018)

Omar Earle (40, years old body found June 11, 2018)
Leon Griffith (31, years old body found June 11, 2018)
Dario Yearwood (27 years old, body found September 7, 2018)

Daniel Griffith (37 years old, body found September 7, 2018)
Andrew Haylett (34 years old, body found October 25, 2018)
Monique Brown (23 years old, body found October 25, 2018)

Nancy Hardy (72 years old, body found November 28, 2018)
Barbara Findley (48 years old, body found December 5, 2018)
Demar Stennett (20 years old, body found January 5, 2019)

& these are only some.

I

HERE

TRANSLATION OF A JAMAICAN CURSE

'Guh dead ah bush!'

Or else, you could say: *may death wait for you*
in the undergrowth, the understory; may you drag yourself
there, like a wounded dog towards the hem of hedges.
And there, where is the darkness, where is the furnace
of worms, where are the fallen leaves, may the world
above you be a buzzing, colourless thing. May you feel
the earth's rhythm and weather and wear; may you think
'of all places I have ended here'.

Here that is the unplotted plot, the intriguing
twist of vines, the messy dialogue – just listen
how the leaves *uh* & *ah* & *er* nonstop.

> The 'horse dead & cow fat' is here, as well
> the sob story, the tall story & the same old story.
> Whomever did tell you there was two sides

to every story is someone who don't know the true
nature of stories. Try two hundred, or two thousand,
& they are all here. A web of Nansi story hangs thick

> between the trees. The original accounts
> of witnesses are here, as well a careful record
> of all subsequent changes; you may compare.

The long bench is here, perfectly sized, that you might hear
the long story that will not be cut short. Here where is
the hard luck story, the likely & unlikely stories,

> & all the tales that were put on shelves,
> 'Oh,' the teller had said, waving a hand,
> 'that's a whole other story!' Well, my dear,

they are here – in the complication of roots, in the dirtiness
of dirt. Are there stories you have heard about Jamaica?
Well here are the stories underneath.

the invention of doors (which was the invention of the outdoors);

before the invention of town (which was the invention of the outskirts, the peripheries);

before the invention of gates (which was the invention of the outside, the outsider, the barbarians in wait. It should be noted there are many kinds of gates & many kinds of barbarians; in Jamaica, the gates of Kingston produce a kind offensively called 'butu');

Here that was here before the invention of keys (which was the invention of a lie – the world was somewhere else & we could close a door to it);

before the invention of curtains (which was the invention of spying nervously in your own back yard, at night after the dogs bark, the motion-sensor lights come on, you can see everything except what is behind the crotons);

before the invention of burglar bars (which was the invention of an accidental art installation in Hope Pastures, Jamaica – a house surrounded entirely by steel, like a dollhouse in a birdcage);

before the invention of boundaries (which was the invention of fences, and also the invention of countries – countries being the invention of men wearing clothes the colour of trees, patrolling the arbitrary lines, the dark promise of their rifles);

before the invention of stamps (which was the invention of
bureaucracy, which was the invention of embassies, which was the
invention of old women gathered hopelessly on Hope Road, the
quartz of their sweat glistening on their foreheads)

& here that was here before the invention of here (which was the
invention of there)

before the invention of distance (which was the invention of
letters, tear stained, held tight in the hands of the women gathered
hopelessly on Hope Road)

before the invention of place (which was the invention of the world
as we know it now)

before the invention of time (which was at once the invention of
now & the invention of after & the invention of before).

Here that is here in the now

& that was here in the before

& that shall be here in the after

that shall hold our bodies, our cities, our outdated stamps

in its endless cycle of green & brown & flower & thorn & stone.

Here where blossom the orchids, two hundred
        & twenty in variety. Some have adapted to bone
dry places, to being purple amongst the stone.

        Here where blossom Jamaican Ladies
of the Night, I mean the flowers –
        their petals, the colour of weddings,

their perfume, the scent of parlours.
        There is much that blossoms in these bushes
& much that rots, like Jamaican ladies of the night -

        I no longer mean the flowers. Here
where grows the Hog Apple, the Hog Money. Here
        where wild hogs rut at the roots of things.

The trees, sometimes, are grunting.
        Here where you can find the Tuna.
Here, the Monkey's Hand, the Cow's Tongue,

such things seem not to belong
        to bushes, but they are as much a part
as the Bullock's Heart, the Dog's Tail –

        as much a part as the broken
bottles & burnt cars. Is that
        the right way to say it? Especially

here? Should I have said: *de heap*
          of bruk bokkle & de plenty bun up cyar?
Here that cannot be held

by the small arms of language.
          Here that cannot be held
by the small arms of English.

          Here that cannot be held by the English.
          But how they tried!
Here is where they found Nanny

          or where Nanny found them,
where you might find her still – if you believe
          in kumina, the never-dead of spirts.

Nanny – do you know her story? Her peculiar ability
          to catch bullets? & where? Some say
she could even shoot them back

          but I think this was just a metaphor
for the magnificent stink of her farts,
          that coming across a whiteman

          she could lift up her frocktail
          & clear the bush of English.
Here where is the inscrutability. The wild

          & passionate uproar. Here
where is the horror! The horror!
          Here where you might find the war.

Here where blossoms the knife,
here where blossoms the blade,
        here where glistens the blood.

The Wild Mint grows here, & the Wild
            Pawpaw, & the Wild Sage,
& the Wild Caesar Obeah. So much wildness

        can be found here where creeps
the Cerassee, the Love Bush that strangles trees.
        Here where shines the Raw Moon –

        'Raw Moon' being folk etymology. Original word,
Ramoon. Here where you will find
        the much improved

names of things – the slow greening & rootsing
            of Latin; 'Semen contra' becomes Semi-contract,
'Sempervivum' becomes 'Simple Bible'

        becomes, 'Sinkle Bible' – let the trees
say Amen. Here where blossoms the Ginger,
        here where blossoms the danger.

        Here where you must pray
against the loud bark of Cedar,
        seek God in the orchids

ask help of Archangels, though here
            Archangels are only flowers,
their petals, the colour of weddings,

their perfume, the scent of parlours –
      by which I mean the heavily powdered dead,
this landscape like a wreath laid

      against itself. Here where blossoms the Natto,
here where blossoms the Nettle.
         Here where blossoms the Night.

after EBONY G. PATTERSON'S
'while the dew is still on the roses'

Here where are the bodice (spectacularly
jewelled) & the bodies (spectacularly jewelled).
Observe them – each one a catalogue

of fine sewing: back tack, cross-stitch, tentstitch –
made by women with hands as sure as surgeons
Here where are the hairpins; they glitter

like dew on the roses. Goodison reminds us
to us, all flowers are roses. & here
where is the hair, a braid, dancehall red,

now abandoned as if it had freed itself
from one head duly conked – the Neanderthal pull
of a man. Here where you must bear witness

to what the hair had closed its eye to –
the black cloud of shoes, the sound hymning
between the leaves: *the day thou gavest Lord*

has ended, the darkness falls at thy behest.
Here that is not holy ground, but just a hole
in the ground – the funereal mound.

Here that pulls the tears back into the soft
bodies of boys, & observe them –
their soft & spectacular bodies,

their spectacular bodices, the spectacular
corsets, the spectacular corpses. I want so much
to say this - that our bodies are spectacular

& not the harder truth – that our bodies
are spectacles; our deaths blossom like roses
in the dark garden behind the house.

TO KNOW GREEN FROM GREEN

'And all this in a million shades of green.'
— James Henderson, describing Jamaica.

To know the nearby bushes you must know green from green
know seafoam different from sea, teal different from tea,
& still a million shades between.

Must know hunter different from army different from rifle,
a shot fired causes birds to lift, screaming from the trees,
that 'screamin' is itself a shade of green.

Look: a parakeet, its wings bright against the night,
you must know midnight different from malachite different
from the leathery shade called crocodile,

You must know emerald different from jade; know greens that travel
towards grey – laurel, artichoke, sage. Forest is different from jungle
is different from tree which is itself a shade of green.

You must know India, Paris & Pakistan, that breeze
can rustle language out of leaves: Spanish, Persian, Russian,
& still a million tongues between.

In 1988, a show brought six reindeer to Jamaica. A subsequent hurricane
allowed for their escape into the hills of Portland. Without natural predators,
the population of Jamaican reindeer now stands at approximately 6,000.

Here where run the wild deer –
the Caribbean caribou – does this
surprise you, deer without snow

not even the possibility
of snow? Here, they are like echoes
of a long story – the brutal

history of *dis place*
which is not to say
they are not their own

stories, but that they know, as we do
the tightness of ships
& how to lose whole continents,

& how to be wary
of white men wielding whips,
& how to end up here.

There is such a thing as the perfect storm.
It includes an actual storm & deer
in weak cages & nearby bushes.

How wonderful to escape
into hills that have always been escape.
They are the new maroons. At dawn,

they descend on quiet hooves
to loot from the estates...
            but maybe that isn't fair.

            I should not say 'estates' but farms.
On the 7 o' clock news, a man
            spreads his arms to show

the field of ruined carrots. *Have mercy!*
            Dem nyam every godalmighty ting!
& then

            he faces camera but is looking
somewhere beyond the absent harvest,
            his mind lighting

on memory, *But Jeezas chrise,*
            he breathes, *Dem sooo pretty!*
His face now a curious thing,

            as if ashamed or puzzled
he should recognize such beauty,
            the nobility of their being,

            or accepting too late
this may have been their payment – the price
            of carrots: to be seen.

It is easier to hear the deer
            whose sounds are like doors on old hinges.
At nights, listen,

             the landscape is creaking
as if these bushes open themselves
             to drunk men

just now stumbling home.
             Here, where the wild deer roam. Here,
where dried branches

             may not be dried branches
but the majesty of antlers. Here,
             where white flowers

may not be white flowers, but the blossoming
             of their tails, the strange warning
of deer – we do not see well, but we sense

             you are here, with us in this strange,
strange land. Will you come now
             to the river? Will you teach us

King Alpha's song, & how to survive
             Babylon – how to belong
where we do not belong.

HUSH

Jamaica experiences, on average, 3 earth movements per month.
These are mostly never felt.

Here that cradles the earthquakes;
they pass through the valleys

in waves, a thing like grief,
or groaning that can't be uttered.

Observe the breadfruit leaf,
How it shivers without wind –

this quiet that is not quiet,
this peace that is not peace,

this hush trembling in the landscape;
it is the stifled earthquake.

HERE WHERE IS THE CURE

Here where is the cure for Black Chube,
                 & you had to ask please, Miss Beatrice,
what is 'Black Chube'?

                 & though her words were patient,
her eyes said something different:
                 Is born you born stupid,

or is University turn you fool?
                 Black Chube, she explains
is when woman can't get pregnant.

                 Here you must make adjustment
for the greener sound of things:
                 Blocked Tubes? Black Chube? Same ting.

Here, the strangest cure for stuttering –
                 it goes like this: collect rain water
in a calabash, beat it with a wooden pestle,

                 though some splashing is inevitable,
be careful not to lose much water.
                 Now drink one teaspoon each morning

                 & soon you will find the balance
of your tongue, your speech as smooth as song.
                 Here where is the cure for bellyhat –

& you didn't even have to ask
                 please, Miss Beatrice, what is bellyhat?
You have made adjustment

for the greener sound of things:
not bellyache, not belly-hurt, but bellyhat.
      Now boil Donkey Weed with Colic Mint

in a clean pot. Sweeten, if you must,
      with honey. Here where grows
the Standing Buddy, the Strongback.

      These are cure for 'weak man'
with useless cock. Search-mi-Heart
      is for weak heart. Eyebright

      is for weak eye. Scorn-the-Earth
is medicine for woman,
      its name is its instruction –

plant most heaven bound, its powers
      are diminished if it touches ground.
Here where is the cure for tief.

      Here where is the cure for grudgeful.
Here where is the cure for pickney
      you never want. I dare not write

      these remedies down,
but their ingredients grow here
      amongst the orchids, amongst the deer

that sound like doors
      in the wild & blossoming night. Here
where is the cure.

FOR THE SAKE OF SWEETNESS

Here that burns for the sake of sweetness;
the cane rats are running towards the river.
On evenings like this, the air smelling
of what you might call molasses & I
might call slavery – it is hard to tell
what century we are in. The sky, red
as the bandanas the cane cutters wear
around their faces like bandits, hangs low
as if breathing we might choke on clouds
& its black confetti of ratoon & chaff & tares.

Here, the diminishing miles of crocodiles
who having survived asteroids & the frozen earth
may not survive here where they are reduced
to the smallest yards. There are whole places
in Jamaica named after the crocodiles: Alligator Pond,
Caymanas Estate. You must forgive this – the imprecise names
of places. There were never alligators, there were never caimans,
only the crocodiles who are diminishing, whose swamps
have given way to cement & monument. There was a time
you could put them snout to tail, then snout to tail again
& how they would ring around this island, a thousand mile
circumference of crocodiles, a fierce reptilian halo.
Have you ever observed the shape of Jamaica?
It is a fat crocodile; soon it will be the shape of memory,
the lost miles of history. This is a lament for them –
the crocodiles who lay their fragile eggs in a fragile place.

A PSALM FOR GAY BOYS

'When mi leave, mi haffi go through the bushes, cause if mi did take the road, dem woulda kill me!' – Facebook Live Testimony of [name withheld], 17 year old boy ordered to leave his community on 22 March, 2019

Here that is the confession ● & the truth ● & a softness
amongst the thorns ● where the married men roam ● at night ●
their trousers unzipped ● where we are kissed by the same lips
that curse us ● where we suck the salt softly from each other's
necks ● but only at night ● where we hide ● where we are never
hidden ● where are the shadows ● the shadows being our refuge
& strength ● a present help on the day of judgement ● where is
the judgment ● where is no judgment ● where is the escape ●
but only at night ● when the married men chase us ● & curse
us with the same lips ● where we run to ● where we stop running ●
where men hang their jackets in trees ● where the moon reveals
the shapes of shoulders floating ● like Scott's apostrophe to pain ●
a landscape of strange lynchings ● where is the sobbing ● where is
 the aahing ● where we trace our fingers against each other's bare
& trembling backs ● where we kneel ● where our mouths are full
of things harder than prayers ● where is the away from home ● &
the way home ● & the roadway in the wilderness ● & the way
where there was no way ● where we come to ● again & again ●
& again ● Here that is the limboed land ● a place between
places ● the ends of the earth ● here that is the Hear
my cry ● O Lord ● My Lord ● My God ● Attend now to my needs.

II

SOMETIMES I CONSIDER THE NAMES OF PLACES

10 MICRO-ESSAYS

SOMETIMES I CONSIDER THE NAMES OF PLACES

Sometimes I consider the names of places:

New York, as if York was not enough;

New Orleans, as if Orleans was not enough;

New England, as if England was not enough;

the New World

as if this world was not enough.

There was once a woman from nowhere. That is how Hanna would begin as if it was a fairy tale she was telling and not the story of her grandmother – a woman who had lived in seven countries without ever having moved. And imagine that – the same house, the same stairs, the same clock upon the wall. But outside things were always changing, the armies invading, the borders shifting. Some mornings, without warning, the radio would just up and start speaking a new language. *Babička learned how to be polite in German, and how to be demure in Russian, just so the square jawed men in green uniforms would not rape her. She could describe perfectly the land where she was from. She could not always name the place.*

Sometimes I consider the names of places. New Zealand, as if Zeelandia was not enough. And because the Dutch Explorer, Abel Tasman, had already spent the bounty of his name on Tasmania. At first he called it 'Staten Landt', believing its mountain ranges connected to the southern tip of South America. Argentina, Peru, Chile, New Zealand. Three years later, it was renamed Nova Zeelandia.

In Nova Zeelandia, on the spot of land whose coordinates are 45°52′S 170°30′E is a place that was once called Otepoti, and is still called Otepoti by those with long memory, and would still be written on the maps as 'Otepoti' if it weren't for a Scottish churchman who saw something in the landscape that reminded him of home.

Place name – Dunedin. Old Gaelic word. 'Dun' being the same word as 'fort'. Fort being the same word as 'burgh'. Dunedin, or Fort Edin, or Edin Fort, or Edinburgh. And it doesn't stop there. The town planner is instructed to 'emulate' the Scottish City, as if to make territories out of maps, as if to tame the too-wild landscape, as if to baptize and make good Christians out of trees.

But I love the way that landscapes resist, the poet Bill Manhire tells me. *How they throw up mountains where there should be valleys, and lakes where there should be fields, and rivers where there should be sea.*

These things I know as much as you: how morning comes, that slow brightening of sky; the world revealing itself as outline, the shape of rooves, and birds that oar themselves across the high pink sea; the day that does not yet smell of day; the here that could be anywhere, and every place. It is possible, in that pre-day world – to ignore the specifics, the names of birds or places, the specific shape of rooves – to simply be in the world, wrapped by an unbothered sky.

Sometimes I consider the names of places: The West Indies. Or said another way: Western India

as if India was not enough.

And isn't it incredible that such a name should stick despite all geographic proof to the contrary. And maybe this is what place is – a distorted way of seeing, an insufficient imagining.

Cristobal, como se dice 'Taino' en espanol?   Indio

Cristobal, como se dice 'Carib' en espanol?   Indio

Cristobal, como se dice 'Guanahatabey' en espanol?   Indio

What did it matter, our own names?

We are insufficiently imagined people from an insufficiently imagined place.

PLACE NAME: <u>ORACABESSA</u> –

origins disputed but most likely leave-over from the
Spanish. *Oracabeza*, Golden Head, though what gold was here
other than light glinting off the bay, other than bananas bursting
out from red flowers? Though this too is disputed – not the
flowers – but the origin of bananas; they may have come here with
Columbus on a ship which in 1502 slipped into Oracabessa the way
grief sometimes slips into a room. In those days the sailor tried to
name the island *Santiago*, as if not knowing we already had a name,
in another language, a language whose speakers would soon all die
– though this too is disputed – not the deaths, but the completeness
of genocide. For consider, if you will, such leave-over words as
hurricane; consider *barbecue;* consider *Xaymaca*, land of wood and
water – of wood and water but not of gold. Could someone please
go back in time and tell Columbus, in Taino there is no word
for gold. Christopher Columbus, in Italiano *Cristoforo Colombo*,
en español *Cristóbal Colón*. A teacher once told me '*Colón*' is root
word for colonist, and though I know that was false etymology,
there is some truth to it. Oracabessa – place where you might find
such tranquil villas as *Golden Ridge, Golden Clouds, Goldeneye* –
long-time home of Ian Fleming who sat there on cliff's edge, the
morning's breakfast brought to him by a woman named Doris,
the scent of ackee and crisp-fried breadfruit wafting up to his
nostrils while between his teeth he bit a number 2 pencil, all the
time looking out to sea as if fishing for a story – maybe a man – an
incredible man – let's call him Bond. James Bond. Who knew 007
wasn't actually Scottish, but a barefoot bwoy from St Mary, Jamaica.
Like so many others, he too migrated – the brutish winter cooling
his complexion down to white. Such stories! *Goldfinger, Goldeneye,
the Man with the Golden Gun.* Did you never stop to wonder where

all this gold came from? Did you never stop to ask, what was found in El Dorado? Well, let me tell you: not a nugget, not an ounce of ore – but light gilding the bay, and perhaps bananas, and perhaps ackee, and such language as could summon wind to capsize Columbus's ships – and if that's not gold, then what is?

SO WHAT WILL WE CALL THE THING
BETWEEN PLACES

So what will we call the thing between places? Like hiking up a
mountain – that thing between one village and the next, between
the long sit downs, the stretch between the stretch? What do you
call it – that interruption of miles that might smell of eucalyptus,
that limbo of land when there is nothing left to see, just the same
hills rolling to the same valleys, the same unbothered sky, and that
turn you could swear you already took two miles down the hill is
here again, and you fighting for the same thin air, a pain in your
ankle, the trudging trudge of it all, and too wary to make out of it a
metaphor, something about striving.

Or else like driving, or being driven – the part that is just road and
night and cats-eyes like a scattering of stars – the part where you
sleep.

Or else, like flying across the Atlantic – not the buckle-up or the
take-off, not the meal or the movie, but that lull when the cabin
lights are dimmed and the blankets are drawn –

What is it called – the nameless space between, as if nothing
important happened here. As if no one important happened here.

Sometimes I consider the nameless spaces – the here that was here before the invention of doors or houses or cities, the landscape before it was landscaped, just the easy acres of possibility.

I have read it is possible to hear trees breathing. And that they send messages across a complicated network of roots – warnings of insects, and what defences can be used. And it is possible to observe the slow walk of trees, thought it might take you a thousand years to see them inching across a ridge.

If sometimes it is possible to hear trees breathing, can you also hear them catch their breaths before the violence of place? Because isn't place always a violence – the decimation of trees, the genocide of bees, the dislocation of birds, the cutting, the clearing, the paving, the smoothing, the raising up of cement like giant tombstones over the grave of all that was there before.

WHAT I REMEMBER NOW IS THE CIRCLE
OF THUNDER

What I remember now is the circle of thunder, a roundabout of
rumbling, distant enough that we could pretend for some time
we were not hearing it. I think now about those minutes of denial
– how slow we always are to admit to new things or things we
cannot name. We were town people after all, out of place in that
kind of green field that spreads behind the quick-stick fences of
red dirt roads in rural Jamaica – the kind of fence against which
you might expect to find an old man wearing a straw hat and
waterboots – a farmer of onions or lettuce or even cows – and who,
had he followed us over the fence and into this field, might have
understood the roundabout of rumbling, and could have named it
for us.

We had climbed over the fence on our own and hiked until we
found what seemed a good spot to build a fire. And our laughter
was the sound of the night, and the crackling wood the sound of
the stars. But then came the circle of thunder which was not the
sound of the moon or the galaxies or the trees or anything we knew.
We pretended we did not hear it.

No matter how fierce the hurricane of words or the gales of
laughter, there always comes lull – a suddenness of silence, like
a held breath, or the flatness between waves. And into that lull
stepped the thunder. What the hell is that? And the question, said
out loud, made it impossible for us to persist in denial. We turned
on our flashlights – shone them out into the darkness. From a
distance we could not measure, flaming red eyes stared back at us.

We screamed. Only then did we hear them clearly – the neighing and whinnying. Horses. About a dozen of them. We were in their field. Our fire had disturbed them. The dull thunder around us was their hooves. We outed the fire as quickly as we could, and just as quickly made our way back to the fence and over it.

And what I remember now is the country road stretched out before us, and the night, and our clothes still smelling of smoke. And that we were town people, and that we were out of place, though I never understood then what places meant nor what it meant to be outside them.

To consider the nearby bushes – a stretch of canefield perhaps, or the crotons behind the house – is to consider the nameless places, or perhaps the placeless places. It is to consider the nonspecific 'here' – a here that could be everywhere, or maybe nowhere.

III

IN NEARBY BUSHES

The community of Mount Peace in Hanover is in mourning after the decomposed body of 20-year-old xxxxxx xxxxx, who has been missing for the past two weeks, was found buried in a shallow grave in Kew Top, near her community last Sunday.

Reports are that xxxxxx left her home on January 27 to visit her twin sister in Montego Bay. It is said that she left her sibling's home to return to her parish on February 12, but she did not arrive at her destination. Despite getting assistance from the police to search for her, no one was able to locate her. During the time of xxxxxx disappearance, friends and loved ones also took to social media to seek information that could help them to locate her and pray for her safe return.

However, things took a turn for the worse when a group of family members and friends from her community saw dogs fighting in nearby bushes.

JAMAICA STAR, FEBRUARY 27, 2018

The community of **Mount Peace** in Hanover **is in mourning** after the decomposed body of 20-year-old xxxxxx xxxxx, who has been missing for the past two weeks, was found buried in a shallow grave in Kew Top, near her community last Sunday.

Reports are that xxxxxx left her home on January 27 to visit her twin sister in Montego Bay. It is said that **she left** her sibling's home **to return** to her parish **on February 12,** but **she did not arrive at her destination.** Despite getting assistance from the police to search for her, no one was able to locate her. During the time of xxxxxx disappearance, **friends and loved ones** also took to social media to seek information that could help them to locate her and **pray for her safe return.**

However, things took **a turn for the worse** when a group of family members and friends from her community saw dogs fighting **in nearby bushes.**

JAMAICA STAR, FEBRUARY 27, 2018

The community of Mount Peace in Hanover is in mourning after the decomposed body of 20-year-old xxxxxx xxxxx, who has been missing for the past two weeks, was found buried in a shallow grave in Kew Top, near her community last Sunday.

Reports are that xxxxxx left her home on January 27 to visit her twin sister in Montego Bay. It is said that she left her sibling's home to return to her parish on February 12, but she did not arrive at her destination. Despite getting assistance from the police to search for her, no one was able to locate her. During the time of xxxxxx disappearance, friends and loved ones also took to social media to seek information that could help them to locate her and pray for her safe return. However, things took a turn for the worse when a group of family members and friends from her community saw dogs fighting in nearby bushes.

JAMAICA STAR, FEBRUARY 27, 2018

The community of Mount Peace in Hanover is in mourning after the decomposed body of 20-year-old xxxxxx xxxxx, who has been missing for the past two weeks, was found buried in a shallow grave in Kew Top, near her community last Sunday.

Reports are that xxxxxx left her home on January 27 to visit her twin sister in Montego Bay. It is said that she left her sibling's home to return to her parish on February 12, but she did not arrive at her destination. Despite getting assistance from the police to search for her, no one was able to locate her. During the time of xxxxxx disappearance, friends and loved ones also took to social media to seek information that could help them to locate her and pray for her safe return.

However, things took a turn for the worse when a group of family members and friends from her community saw dogs fighting in nearby bushes.

JAMAICA STAR, FEBRUARY 27, 2018

The community of Mount Peace in Hanover is in mourning after the decomposed body of 20-year-old xxxxxx xxxxx, who has been missing for the past two weeks, was found buried in a shallow grave in Kew Top, near her community last Sunday.

Reports are that xxxxxx left her home on January 27 to visit her twin sister in Montego Bay. It is said that she left her sibling's home to return to her parish on February 12, but she did not arrive at her destination. Despite getting assistance from the police to search for her, no one was able to locate her. During the time of xxxxxx disappearance, friends and loved ones also took to social media to seek information that could help them to locate her and pray for her safe return.

However, things took a turn for the worse when a group of family members and friends from her community saw dogs fighting in nearby bushes.

JAMAICA STAR, FEBRUARY 27, 2018

That this should be your death – walking so simple this last stretch that will stretch into eternity, thinking nothing more than the emptiness of your fridge, and the cupboards, and what feat of magic might produce this evening's meal. And the road so straight and innocent, don't even curl the way some road curl like serpent so walking it you have a sense of evil which is just good manners – the salutation of roads: *Good evening, most gracious wayfarer, most excellent of trodders, mind sharp! Cause I is the kind of road that will fuck you up.*

But you wasn't thinking no thought so deep. You was just walking simple, step by weary step, hands in your pocket holding the key to a door whose threshold you would never know again. And the magnificent breadfruit tree is just an area of darkness. You think this: how shapeless is the night. And then the night reveals its shape. Look - it have a time in everybody's life when don't care how close home is, it so far from Peace.

A hand over your mouth, your scream muffled into an
mmmmmmmmmmm. And all the wait you did wait for a familiar
face to reveal itself, to say, *is just me! Is only me!* You coulda wait till
thy kingdom come.

And the hand of night is on your mouth

and a weight of shadow is pulling you.

And the here of road and breadfruit tree slips away. And 'There'
which you thought a place impossible to reach, available only to
others, or to the faded past of photographs – your fingers tracing
the Rockefeller Tower in New York perhaps, the nostalgic whisper:
I was there.

But now is the thereness of stone and leaf and macca,

the there stink of gullies and sour food and dead dogs.

The thereness of nearby bushes.

And you think, maybe if you close your eyes, you can sleep it off.
Sleep away this useless rage. Wake up in another book, on a kinder
page.

II.I

This is what happens on the morning after your death:

a rooster flutters up to a wall. You see neither rooster nor wall but
are certain of the clumsiness of feathers, the fact of rough concrete,
the wall unpainted, unfinished, like the island from whose earth it
seems to rise.

You are as aware of the rooster as if you were that rooster, the dawn
in your throat like a wave of morning sickness. You strut out as if
walking a plank.

This is what happens, and what will happen every day after: a cock
crows and not no bad tidings neither. That, at least, would have
been something – the world nodding at this that has happened. But
the sound was just the beginning of ordinary - the unbothered day
- the night turning its back to you.

How unspectacular, this business of dying, as if any and anybody
could do it.

On the morning after your death, and then the next, and then the
next, a cock crows, a strangled sound that believes it alone pushes
the stars and the quiet back, calls forth the magnificent breadfruit
tree that steps out of the night like a watchman returning home.

And death which had seemed a thing so dark and far away, is
revealed now as splendid, and here – the here which is jungle &
tree, which is crocodile and parakeet, which is rifle and army, and
the million shades between. You had not imagined death as a thing
so wide, so full of acres and sky.

III

Already the worms are rising, pulling towards you, towards the thing you once considered you: the body. You had a heart; it stopped. Then things began to happen. There are words for these things. The words would not fit on your tongue if you still had a tongue to use: *Pallor Mortis, Algor Mortis, Rigor Mortis.*

Already the worms are rising, as if towards the straw of your body – body being the wrong word. There are words for what your body has become: *Corpse. Carcass. Cadaver.* You, a curious county of decay. You had a heart. It stopped. But the thing that was your body did not stop. It only began to do new things. There are words for these things: *Livor Mortis. Autoloysis. Putrefecation.*

A cell now eats itself. The self now eats itself. The body grows sour, like a green fruit. If only you had a tongue to taste the green fruit of yourself. If only you had a nose to smell what you have become, to smell the weighted waft of yourself, proof that you exist in air, that you are becoming the air, that you bear the flies that come towards the harvest of yourself. How you have become this strange thing – a beacon to flying and crawling insects.

Already the worms are rising. Already parts of your body are returning to earth, which is to say you are becoming the earth, and the things of the earth. You are the air, and the ground, and the things that rise to meet you.

IV

This is how to lie completely still, even for days.
This is how to become a perch for crows.
This is how to love a johncrow.
This is how to love the small wind, the air as disturbed by wings.
This is the coming of the johncrow, the johncrow that lands on your
broken head just so.
These are her pink feet against your cheek. A soft, weak thing, like
the hand of a child. It surprises you.
Had you imagined those feet as strong as eagles'? Had you
imagined them able to lift up small cows? Were you prepared for
the brown of the johncrow's eyes or the fact of her eyelashes? Had
you imagined the luminosity of her underwings – that the johncrow
is a dark cloud with her own silver lining?

Loud explosions sounding like gunshots were heard coming from the direction where the men were. Constable Everald Thomas said that as a result of this, he and his fellow officers were forced to take cover and he returned the fire. The men, however, made good their escape in nearby bushes.

FROM JAMAICA SUPREME COURT
CRIMINAL APPEAL NO 63/2009

during the shootout, the unidentified gunman was shot and killed. The 16-year-old student was shot and injured and a third man who was also involved in the shooting was seen making his escape in nearby bushes.

MCKOY'S NEWS, JANUARY 30, 2018

While the police were in the process of assisting him to the hospital, they reportedly came under heavy gunfire from armed men hiding in nearby bushes.

LOOP JAMAICA, JANUARY 1, 2018

Loud explosions sounding like gunshots were heard coming from the direction where the men were. Constable Everald Thomas said that as a result of this, he and his fellow officers were forced to take cover and he returned the fire. The men, however, made good their escape in nearby bushes.

FROM JAMAICA SUPREME COURT
CRIMINAL APPEAL NO 63/2009

during the shootout, the unidentified gunman was shot and killed. The 16-year-old student was shot and injured and a third man who was also involved in the shooting was seen making his escape in nearby bushes.

MCKOY'S NEWS, JANUARY 30, 2018

While the police were in the process of assisting him to the hospital, they reportedly came under heavy gunfire from armed men hiding in nearby bushes.

LOOP JAMAICA, JANUARY 1, 2018

Loud explosions sounding like gunshots were heard coming from the direction where the men were. Constable Everald Thomas said that as a result of this, he and his fellow officers were forced to take cover and he returned the fire. The men, however, made good their **escape** in nearby bushes.

FROM JAMAICA SUPREME COURT
CRIMINAL APPEAL NO 63/2009

during the shootout, the unidentified gunman was shot and killed. The 16-year-old student was shot and injured and a third man who was also involved in the shooting was seen making his **escape** in nearby bushes.

MCKOY'S NEWS, JANUARY 30, 2018

While the police were in the process of assisting him to the hospital, they reportedly came under heavy gunfire from armed men **hiding in nearby bushes.**

LOOP JAMAICA, JANUARY 1, 2018

Loud explosions sounding like gunshots were heard coming from the direction where the men were. Constable Everald Thomas said that as a result of this, he and his fellow officers were forced to take cover and he returned the fire. The men, however, made good their escape in nearby bushes.

FROM JAMAICA SUPREME COURT
CRIMINAL APPEAL NO 63/2009

during the shootout, the unidentified gunman was shot and killed. The 16-year-old student was shot and injured and a third man who was also involved in the shooting was seen making his escape in nearby bushes.

MCKOY'S NEWS, JANUARY 30, 2018

While the police were in the process of assisting him to the hospital, they reportedly came under heavy gunfire from armed men hiding in nearby bushes.

LOOP JAMAICA, JANUARY 1, 2018

V

'From the pockets of thieves' is how you might write the beginnings
of this place – your own made up story. A thief, his pockets, and
the rustle of seeds. Maybe he had procured them from the trade of
a mother's cow. Not his own mother of course - one he had stolen.
You mean to say the cow was stolen, not the mother. The mother
being a woman suddenly without a cow. And without a proper law
to lean on. The mother will beat her children as if they were thieves.
She will beat them until their own tears clean the white of hunger
that stains their mouths. And the thief, who you now imagine on
the run from Babylon, or else a crowd from whose pockets he had
stolen, reaches into his own and throws the seeds. Look how before
him sprouts the nearby bushes. Even on gravel. Even on rock. Even
on the fourth floor of an office building in New Kingston. Always
the thieves escape in nearby bushes. Impenetrable by police – like
a leave-over of Nanny's magic. How strange that you end up here,
landscape of bruk bokkle and plenty bun of cyar, landscape of old
tires and old shoes. Place you did only hear bout on the RJR news.
Bad news. You, in Jamaica's hidden parish.

V I

Sometimes just so the bushes shiver, like it could be the wind but is
not the wind. Nor the pause in the middle
of Eddie Baugh's baritone
nor the beginning of God clearing his own deep throat:
take off your shoes this is holy ground.
Is just the sign of some other life behind the leaves, another world
inside this world. And sometimes, just so after this shiver of leaves,
a rooster will step out, that forward lurching march that make birds
look foolish – the rooster, like a God without its myth, like a useless
thing without the day around it pinkening.

The body, found earlier this month, was burnt beyond recognition with only a hand with a wrist watch visible. A motor car believed to be owned by the man was also found in nearby bushes.

RJR NEWS, AUGUST 11, 2017

VII.I

If you could move over the breadfruit leaf – the one that has turned the colour of what an uncle who migrated calls 'autumn', you would find a skeleton. The skeleton of an SUV. Hidden just so, under a simple leaf. And it would not surprise you, the magic of nearby bushes, this turning of things into nothing.

The SUV, once green, has turned the colour you refuse to call autumn. After all! In every country, leaf drop and dead in the same colour. The vehicle is only the colour of dead leaves, as if it too has fallen, which it has.

BMW. X5. You used to spot them in this island's traffic. You used to read the name as 'times five'. A multiplication. Driven by a man who wanted all walk-foot gyal like you to know how multiply rich he was. How multiply important. A man who in manner is not unlike your uncle – your uncle who migrated and sends pictures of himself beside BMWs, as if to suggest proximity is ownership. As if to suggest he has been multiplied abroad. You have asked him, *you think mi did born when mi mother did gone market?* You know the car is only one he passes while walking to work at Dunkin' Donuts.

But how he marvels now at the seasons – the autumnal colours. He has used this word – 'autumnal' – and you think, maybe he has been multiplied after all, or at least added on to. How are we increased if not with words? But where is the driver of the X5? All that remains is a skeleton. Did he wait patient at a traffic light? Did it never turn from red to green? Did it turn too late? How awful, the changing of seasons on a road.

It is always autumn in the nearby bushes. This sentence pleases you. It makes the bushes seem far away, like a place you have migrated to – a place that knows the lessening sun, the increasing dark, the beautiful fall of things.

VIII

Something is kicking in this island's womb. Something overdue.
Seismologists say it will be Port Royal Version 2. Or 1907 Version
2. When the earth moved today, it felt like you – the rattling of
yourself into something new.

To consider the earthquake - the terror that waits inside this
island's womb, is to consider the whatnots, how they squat across
our living rooms. It is to consider their shelves of precarious dogs -
such odd porcelain treasures - made in China and dearly loved by
women like your grandmother.

To consider the earthquake, is to consider the useless faith of
whatnots, the useless faith of your grandmother who even now
prays that you are coming home. And you will. But you will come
as a great rattling of things.

This is what happened in Port Royal: a man was standing on what
he knew as ground. In just seconds he was drowning. To drown on
your own acre of land – isn't that something!

To consider the earthquake is to consider the man who drowns
on his own acre of land; it is to consider the sound of dogs not
barking but tinkling; it is to consider how porcelain tumbles; it is to
consider the future as rubble, the way your grandmother's faith will
become rubble.

Because the rudeboys have started speaking with sweet yankee
accents. Because they call old women in Foreign. Because the
women know it is a scam, but who else to talk to on winter
evenings?

Because a sense of sun can pass through a phone, can warm the
bone, drain the purse. Because Obama never like it one bit. Cause
the Governor Ginnal tired of looking foolish. He looks down on
his small, unnecessary hands.

Because the Governor Ginnal has a given a throne speech, and you
didn't even know there was a throne in Jamaica House, and if it was
made of gold, and encrusted with fake diamonds like the Gucci
belts worn by the rudeboys who are the cause of all this trouble.

Because the rudeboys are getting too brazen. Because they walk bout town in bright yellow denim, tight around their small hips, their Calvin Klein boxers showing. Because of their bright yellow sneakers that match.

Because of something they call 'flossing'. What your mother might call 'butuism'. What your granny might call 'boogooyaga'. Because the rudeboys now drive Benzes, though Benz don't stop them from butu. Because of something Rex Nettleford said.

Because they killed a rudeboy in front of white people. Is all well and good to kill people, but not in front of white people. Not right there at the airport. Their final image of Jamaica was Jamaica. Because they did not consider the tourist dollar.

Because Montego Bay is no longer Montego Bay. Because the town getting too hot. Because they now calling it *Scamaica*.

And not because you dead. And not because you are bloating. Not because you are bursting. Not because the larvae squirm inside your skin. Not because a rudeboy has killed you. You were not killed in front of white people. You were killed in the good and proper way. But still, because of the rudeboys.

Because of their bright yellow denim. Because of their diamond encrusted belts. Because of their sweet Yankee accents. It is now a State of Emergency.

Now the soldiers are marching. Left and right. Left and Right. They march right by your body. They are looking for the rudeboys. They are looking for justice. They are not looking for you.

X

That of all places, you should end up here. Here where are the severed heads. Here where are the broken hymens. Here where the four girls were never found, and here where a girl was found in an igloo, chopped into small pieces, like goat. Here where is the never-reach-home. Here where are the lost cellphones. Here, the undialed numbers. Here where is the no signal. Here where are the things that grip – the anger, the shock, the calloused hands. Here where are the undergarments lost in the undergrowth. Here where are the stories lost in the understory. Here where are the things we can't say in front of white people. Because of the tourist dollar. Here where the unsayable blossoms like orchids, like purple amongst the stone. Here that is the half past midnight. And the never-ending Monday. And the discarded weeks. Here where we are pulled into things we cannot speak.

Do you know of Sally in the Woods, or another story like it? The
murdered girl that roams the forest – this useless energy of ghosts.
I mean to ask: what shall be the content of your haunting, what
question will sustain the afterlife? Will it be the usual 'why me?'
and 'how come'? And will it move spectral amongst the bushes, like
the white deer, or Sally at midnight? Or is this just the false way we
imagine the dead – as beautifully hooved, or like vapour, and always
asking the hard questions left us – this way we burden the lifeless
with our most lively fears.

Look – I did not want to admit this, but I found you – the rotting
fact of you – in a newspaper article. And then I looked you up on
Facebook. I saw pictures of your great love – the beautiful fawn of a
child. And you were always smiling. It did not look like the picture
in the newspaper, which wasn't really of you, but of men in masks,
the yellow investigative tape, a backdrop of bushes – the bushes
that held a body we could only imagine. I imagined the body of my
cousin – my cousin who is still alive but who locks the useless doors
so tight because she too had been dragged into nearby bushes. I did
not know you. I do not know that my breath had any right to catch,
or my heart to stop, or myself to wake up these past few nights
haunted by the dream of you.

In the dream you are my cousin. In the dream you are a white deer.
You stand beautiful in the dawn. You are hidden by the mist. You
run away on thin hooves.

XII

What you wouldn't do for the clarity which follows rain, or rather
hurricanes, the ones that come bearing names of old women:
Iris, Irene, Inez – the awful eyes of them – like the women from
church who look down from unloving heights, and who shake their
tambourines with the energy of thunder, and whose tongues roar like
wind across a landscape.
But after the hurricane, always a clarity. Or rather a clearance. The
land presents itself like a secret tired of being kept. So that looking
out you never know before things was so near, like Last Days
vision – this sudden abundance of seeing, like what Sister Inez always
prophesy when she get in spirit, when she shabba and she shekkeh
and then she say
all what is done in secret will come to light
and all hidden things shall be revealed.
In the Last Days.
And it kinda strange to now be the secret and hidden thing – to be of
such gravity, which is to say, of the grave, however shallow – to be a
thing waiting on Revelation.

Anger and shock gripped the community yesterday after gunmen kicked open the door to the house where the girl and her family reside, and dragged her to nearby bushes where she was raped.

JAMAICA OBSERVER, MAY 2, 2014

he said that it was sometime after 10 o'clock Monday night when their Irwin home was invaded by the two gunmen. The criminals gathered all five females, took away their cellphones and led them into nearby bushes.

STARBROEK NEWS, SEPTEMBER 29 2012

XIII.I

Soon now.
Soon they will find you, or the thing you once considered you,
the body, its parts scattered like seed. There are words for what
you have become, and words for what has been done: mechanical
asphyxiation, Ligature bindings, multiple areas of haemorrhage
bilaterally in the conjunctiva, abrasions to the anterior cervical,
trauma and abrasions to the genitalia, broken proximal phalanx.
The words mean nothing to you. What you really want to say is
bruise. And what you really want to say is *broken*. And what you
really want to say is *bone*, and *neck*, and *pussy*.

XIII.II

Say what? Is really that them send you go school to learn?
See, even dead some things cannot be said – some words cannot be
uttered. As if language is more violent than murder. As if your body
is more indecent than rape.
And what you really want to say is: Mi never go school to learn
how fi dead neither! Or how to spread out and be a thing for the
convenience of man,
a man who could just hold you so
could just drag you so
could turn yu pussy inside out
just so
just cause him did feel to – just cause today him don't want to back
him own fist – just cause him did want something warm and soft to
go inside and you just happen to be close by
the moment when him cocky was hard, and he don't feel no need to
ask you or lyrics you or tell you how him did get lost in the brown
of your eyes, or how you shape good

XIII.III

Cause woman is disposable as that,
and this thing that has happened is common,
common,
common as stone and leaf and breadfruit tree.
You should have known. You did always walk on this island aware
of the nearby bushes
the nearby bruises.

The community of Mount Peace in Hanover is in mourning after the decomposed body of 20-year-old xxxxxx xxxxx, who has been missing for the past two weeks, was found buried in a shallow grave in Kew Top, near her community last Sunday.

Reports are that xxxxxx left her home on January 27 to visit her twin sister in Montego Bay. It is said that she left her sibling's home to return to her parish on February 12, but she did not arrive at her destination. Despite getting assistance from the police to search for her, no one was able to locate her. During the time of xxxxxx disappearance, friends and loved ones also took to social media to seek information that could help them to locate her and pray for her safe return.

However, things took a turn for the worse when a group of family members and friends from her community saw dogs fighting in nearby bushes.

JAMAICA STAR, FEBRUARY 27, 2018

XIV

That this should be your death – walking so simple this last stretch
that will stretch into eternity...
And now is the here of stone and leaf and macca,

the here stink of gullies and sour food and dead dogs.

the hereness of nearby bushes.

And you think, maybe if you close your eyes, you can sleep it off.
Sleep away this useless rage. Wake up in another book, on a kinder
page.